Two Women Astronauts

by Ian Gale

PEARSON

Scott
Foresman

Editorial Offices: Glenview, Illinois • Parsippany, New Jersey • New York, New York
Sales Offices: Needham, Massachusetts • Duluth, Georgia • Glenview, Illinois
Coppell, Texas • Ontario, California • Mesa, Arizona

ISBN: 0-328-13480-5

CONTENTS

Chapter 1
Two Special Women

What do scientists do? They try to figure out how things work and why things happen. A scientist might attempt to understand patterns in the weather or help find cures for illnesses. Scientists have skills that can lead them to interesting careers.

For two American women, careers as scientists led them all the way to outer space! Dr. Sally Ride, from California, and Dr. Mae Jemison, from Alabama, made history when they **ventured** into outer space.

In 1983 Sally Ride became the first American woman in space, while Mae Jemison made history in 1992 when she became the first African American woman to travel into space.

Sally Ride and Mae Jemison are two famous former **astronauts** who worked for the National Aeronautics and Space Administration (NASA).

Chapter 2
Meet Dr. Sally Ride

When Sally Ride was a youngster growing up in California, she wasn't interested in traveling to space, after all, the space program hadn't yet started. Like many other children her age, Sally was interested in playing sports and having fun with her friends.

In addition to participating in and enjoying tennis and other sports, Sally developed an avid interest in science. In fact, she was so interested in science that she chose it as a major subject in college.

Sally studied and earned several degrees in physics from Stanford University in California. It was at Stanford that Sally would take her first step toward becoming an astronaut.

It was an advertisement in the university's newspaper that caught Sally's attention. The ad explained that NASA was hiring astronaut candidates for its new space shuttle program. NASA particularly needed people who knew about **astronomy** and other sciences.

Sally was intrigued by the thought of becoming an astronaut and training with NASA, so she decided to apply. Competition for the job was extremely tough. More than one thousand other women, along with many thousands of men, sent applications to NASA. From among all of the applicants, NASA reduced the list of possible candidates to just thirty-five people— and Sally was one of them!

She was required to take many tests, and she went through an arduous interview process at the Johnson Space Center in Houston, Texas. But Sally made the team! Soon she would be an astronaut—a mission specialist to be exact. That's the position she would be training for.

It would be a year, however, before Sally would be ready to take her first flight into outer space aboard the space shuttle *Challenger*.

During training Sally became the expert on the Remote Manipulator System. This system is a giant robotic arm that is used to move cargo in the shuttle's payload bay and to pick up and release **satellites** that the shuttle is placing in orbit.

After one year of rigorous training, Sally was eligible for assignment as a mission specialist on a space shuttle flight crew. She wasn't assigned to a shuttle mission immediately, however. First, as part of additional training, she was a member of the support crew of other shuttle flights and worked in NASA's mission control as a capsule communicator, or CAPCOM. In this role, Sally was responsible for communicating information and **data** from scientists and other experts to the shuttle crew in space.

Finally, Sally's chance to be a shuttle crewmember arrived. Sally Ride was about to become the first American female astronaut!

It was the summer of 1983, and the space shuttle *Challenger* was cleared for lift-off. Commander Bob Crippen led Sally and the other *Challenger* astronauts into the special room where they would put on their protective spacesuits and prepare to board the space shuttle.

After the crew was strapped in place and the shuttle was ready to go, the engines roared. Sally Ride was on her way into outer space. Her journey into space and back lasted six days, two hours, and twenty-four minutes.

Challenger lift-off, 1983

Chapter 3
Meet Dr. Mae Jemison

Mae Jemison was born in Alabama in 1956. When Mae was three years old, her family moved to Chicago, Illinois. There, Mae spent a great deal of time at the public library reading books and learning about science. She also loved languages and, over the years, learned Russian, Japanese, and Swahili—an African language. From an early age, however, Mae was determined to become a scientist.

At the age of sixteen, Mae entered Stanford University, where she earned degrees in chemical engineering and African American studies. Mae then went on to become a medical doctor. She studied at and received her medical degree from Cornell University in New York.

Mae was very interested in helping people in disadvantaged countries, so she joined the Peace Corps, an organization that works to help individuals in developing countries who want to build a better life for themselves, their children, and their communities. As a member of the Peace Corps, Mae traveled to the African nations of Sierra Leone and Liberia. She worked as a doctor providing medical care to the people there.

When Mae returned to the United States, she practiced medicine in California. However, she missed working in other scientific fields, so she applied for a mission specialist position at NASA.

Dr. Mae Jemison,
Astronaut

In 1987 Mae Jemison was accepted into NASA's space training program. For the next five years, Mae trained and worked on many projects at NASA. It was very hard work, but Mae was excited at the prospect of making history. She would be the first African American woman in space.

In 1992 Mae took her first journey into space aboard the space shuttle *Endeavour*. Mae's job on that mission was to help conduct experiments in space. Mae's knowledge of science and medicine also helped her to experiment on herself! For example, **biofeedback** is information obtained from monitoring your body and then using this information to control brain waves and body processes, such as heart rate and blood pressure. Mae used biofeedback to help her overcome space motion sickness.

Dr. Mae Jemison, September, 1992

Mae also experimented with frog eggs on her shuttle mission in space. Scientists know how long it takes a frog to develop from an egg into an adult frog here on Earth. They didn't know whether frog eggs would develop at the same rate in outer space as they do on Earth.

Mae conducted her experiments on frog eggs for the eight days of the shuttle mission and discovered that frog eggs do, indeed, develop at the same rate.

In total, Mae helped conduct more than forty different experiments during her space journey.

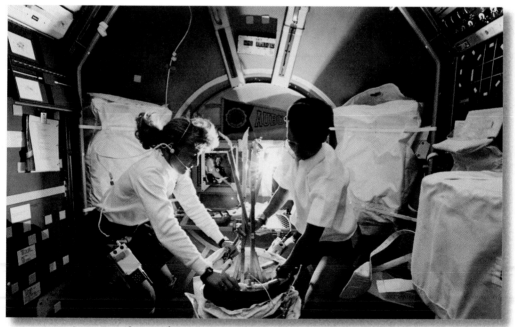

Jan Davis and Mae Jemison set up an experiment on the space shuttle.

After her *Endeavour* mission, Mae left NASA and became a college professor. She also became director of the Jemison Institute at Dartmouth College in New Hampshire, where scientists and experts from all over the world gather to work on technology that will help people in developing countries.

Mae Jemison has worked as a scientist, doctor, and an astronaut. She has even written a book about her life. *Find Where the Wind Goes: Moments from My Life* tells the story of Mae's life and how she fulfilled her dreams.

Whatever career Mae Jemison chooses for herself in the future, she will always look back proudly at her efforts and accomplishments in becoming the first African American woman in space.

15

Chapter 4
Women in Space

The two women you've just read about have both made history. Dr. Sally Ride was the first American woman in space, and Dr. Mae Jemison was the first African American woman in space.

Other women have also traveled into outer space and made history. A Russian woman, Valentina Tereshkova, was the very first woman in space, while Kathryn Sullivan from New Jersey became the first American woman to walk in space. Interestingly, Sally Ride was a member of the same shuttle flight crew as Kathryn Sullivan when Sullivan took her spacewalk. It was Sally Ride's second shuttle flight.

In 1993 Ellen Ochoa became the first Hispanic American woman to travel to outer space, and a year later Chiaki Mukai was the first Japanese woman in space.

American Eileen Collins became the first woman to take command of a spacecraft—she was Shuttle Commander of *Discovery* in 1999.

WOMEN IN SPACE

1959 — Geraldine Cobb is the first woman to pass the tests for the United States' Mercury astronaut training program.

1963 — Valentina Tereshkova from Russia becomes the first woman in space.

Sally Ride becomes the first American woman in space.

1983 —

1984 — Kathryn Sullivan becomes first American woman to walk in space.

1992 — Mae Jemison becomes the first African American woman in space.

1999 — Eileen Collins becomes the first woman space shuttle commander.

Now Try This

Are You Ready for Take Off?

Imagine you are an astronaut! What would it be like to travel into space on a space shuttle or other spacecraft? Write down your thoughts and feelings. Keep a journal.

Here's How to Do It!

Read the following events. Write a journal page for each one, describing what you think it would be like to experience each event.

- You're blasting off from Earth. How does it feel? What do you see?
- You have eaten and slept in space. What predictions can you make about average people traveling and doing everyday things in space?
- You have been in space for two days. How has your body reacted? How have you adjusted?
- You are orbiting Earth for the second time. What have you seen?
- How has your training prepared you for this work and this journey?

If you wish, share your journal with your classmates.

Glossary

astronauts *n.* persons trained to pilot, navigate, or otherwise participate as crew members of a spacecraft.

astronomy *n.* the study of matter in outer space.

biofeedback *n.* information about one's body and body processes obtained from monitoring devices, and then the use of this information to control brain waves and body processes.

data *n.* factual information

ventured *v.* dared to proceed.

satellites *n.* objects that orbit a planet; often refers to human-made objects that are placed in Earth's orbit.